EDINBURGH SINCE 1900

I *The Royal Scottish Academy, Princes Street, 1949* by Robert
Eadie (1877 — 1954)

II *Princes Street looking west with the North British Hotel in the foreground.* Photograph by Sean Hudson, 1987.

EDINBURGH

SINCE

1900

PAUL HARRIS

LOMOND BOOKS

First published by Archive Publications Ltd 1987
2nd Edition 1988
Reprinted 1998 by Lomond Books
36 West Shore Road
Granton
Edinburgh

Printed in the Republic of Slovenia by Gorenjski Tisk Printing Co., Kranj

previous page: *Band Performance in Princes Street* by William Yule

2.   Seated Woman in Princes Street Gardens by William Yule.

CONTENTS

INTRODUCTION
DAWN OF A NEW CENTURY 13—44
EDINBURGH AT WAR 45—77
AT WORK 71—112
AT PLAY 113—142
FESTIVAL CITY 143—178
THE CHANGING FACE OF THE CITY 179—221
DIAL 999! 222—239

ACKNOWLEDGEMENTS

My thanks to all those who helped with this book and especially to those at *The Scotsman:* Andrew Harton for his enthusiasm; Bill Brady and Susie MacEwan in Photo Sales and all the staff at the Picture Library.
Also my thanks to The Fine Art Society Ltd. who kindly provided the handsome picture used on the cover and XIV; Bourne Fine Art for the D M Sutherland of Portobello Beach (X); Anne Paterson Wallace and the Paterson Family for *Edinburgh from Calton Hill* (IV); Dundee Art Galleries and Museums for *Princes Street in the Rain* (III) and particular thanks to Ian O'Riordan and David Paterson at Edinburgh City Art Centre for their assistance and use of pictures V, VI, VII, XI, XII, XIII and XV. The pencil and wash drawings by William Yule, Ernest Lumsden and W G Burn Murdoch are also from the City Art Centre collection. Thank you also to Barbara Watson at Norfolk Capital Hotels for pictures II and XVI.
The black and white photographs are from *The Scotsman* picture library with the exception of 3, 5, 11, 12, 14, 18, 24, 25, 32, 42, 43, 44, 46, 54, 55, 57, 60, 83, 84, 85, 100, 101, 102, 104 and 131, which all come from the Archive Publications collection as do colour pictures VIII, IX and XVII. Pictures 52 and 65 are courtesy of the *Newcastle Chronicle and Journal.*

Paul Harris
August 1987

INTRODUCTION

It has always seemed to me that the people of Edinburgh are conspicuously better at looking at the outside world than at themselves. I am not saying that they are necessarily averse to self-examination but rather that it simply does not seem to occur to them. Of course, introspection can be a fairly fruitless exercise and such is the general self-confidence of the Edinburger that such activity is not writ large on the solid and dramatic landscape of the city.

Some of the best books about Edinburgh have, not surprisingly, either been written by strangers or by former inhabitants living in self-imposed exile. Robert Louis Stevenson, never able to come to terms with his native city whilst he actually lived here, remembered it fondly and perceptively in *Picturesque Notes* — written in France. Despite the large numbers of writers attracted to the city in the 19th and 20th centuries, none has tackled Edinburgh in fiction with more than moderate success. I have often heard modern day writers animatedly discussing the quest for the Great Edinburgh Novel as if it were some sort of elusive Holy Grail. For Edinburgh is a city of such diversity, such social and economic contrasts and such enormous ranges of interests — and conflicts — that the weaving of all these elements together represents an extraordinary challenge to even the most talented of writers. Although many have tried, few have succeeded as well, in my opinion, as Bruce Marshall in *The Black Oxen* (1972) — albeit written from the south of

France. He achieves considerable success in depicting the social and cultural differences within Edinburgh society. One of his most graphic passages describes the scene in the post-First War Palais de Danse where "a mixed bag of semi-sober advocates, writers to the signet, solicitors to the supreme court, chartered accountants, students and keelies were revolving with a kaleidoscope of typists, instructresses, brickfaced Murrayfield heiresses and lugubrious tarts". Somehow in that brief description all Edinburgh is suddenly there before the reader. In the book the chasms within Edinburgh society are summed up by Flora Goodwillie, the object of young Neil Duncan's desire, in a few pithy objections to the continuing of their liaison:

"You live in Murrayfield and I live at the foot of Leith Walk. Your folk have late dinner and mineses have high tea. You talk educated and I talk common."

Although wordsmiths have patently experienced difficulty in encompassing within the confines of two covers the nature of the great city which is Edinburgh, to my mind photographers, over the years, have succeeded somewhat better. As every newspaper picture editor is aware, a good picture is worth a thousand words. A photograph cannot only show things that have gone like horse trams, cable cars and graceful buildings, which are fascinating enough in themselves, but through the capture of gestures and expressions and the interpretation of the photographer it can give us some feeling of how people actually felt and lived.

4.   The Cowgate, Edinburgh, by Ernest Lumsden (1883—1948).

We are fortunate that the 20th century has been so well chronicled as a result of the increasing availability of camera and film. Of course, today virtually everyone has a camera and has become a photographer — at least of sorts. Probably at least fifty per cent of the film shot is wasted and a further fifty per cent of that is promptly lost or disposed of once processed. Even comparatively recent decades — like the 50s and 60s — are quite inadequately recorded despite the wide availability of the camera. Private photographs of the family tend to survive. Press photographs of Great Events survive. But remarkably little else. Great archives of photographic plates have been destroyed rather than retained and negatives and prints by the thousands have ended up in the refuse. A librarian recently told me of tracking down a major collection of glass plates of the 30s and 40s. Arriving at a house in the suburbs he asked to see the plates. The owner proudly took him through the house and pointed to his new greenhouse — every pane representing one scrupulously cleaned glass plate.

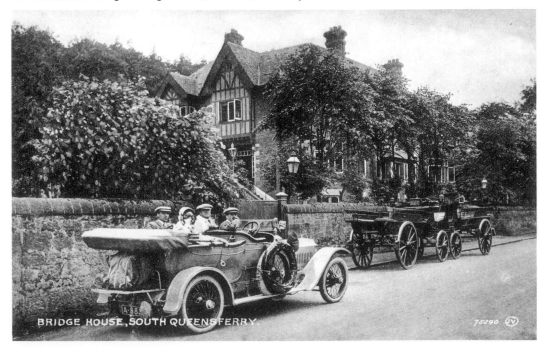

5. A weekend outing at Bridge House, South Queensferry.

Fortunately, today, people are more conscious than ever of heritage generally and the need to preserve what is happening currently for the benefit of later generations. Although much of what is happening today may not seem at all remarkable or noteworthy to us today it will, indubitably, fascinate and amuse our children and grandchildren. We call it nostalgia but I think this is a pejorative term which tends to devalue the activity. We are all interested in where we came from and what happened in our own immediate area in the past. And the recent past seems relatively easier to understand and all the more fascinating — especially when there are still people around who actually remember places and events now gone.

This book is really of the "Gosh, I remember that!" variety. For reasons which psychologists are better able to explain, human beings find it satisfying and fulfilling to reminisce and be reminded of places and things experienced directly or third hand. So, to that activity this book is what the board and cards are to *Trivial Pursuits*. It is something to gather around and use as the basis of a well worn, tried and tested game.

The changes of the 20th century have been so wide ranging that differences in building, transport, design, social activities, work and so on are quite marked enough to make almost any old photograph instantly fascinating. It is here, therefore, that very subjective judgement in selection come into play. All the photographs here I have personally selected — mainly from the archives of *The Scotsman* and *The Evening News* — and I have tried to use certain criteria to establish the credentials of all those used. Do they show us something interesting or unusual which may be different now or do they say something about the process of change? Although one can look through many thousands of photographs, at the end of a day's rummaging through dusty archives there are always a dozen or so images that stay stuck indelibly in the mind. It was those sort of photographs that I was looking for — from the elegantly dressed Victoran ladies at the top of Waverley Steps (15) to the dramatic shot of the fireman of 1987 (233). Then there are images which linger when juxtaposed together — like the Scotsman typesetting machine leaving the building (96) and the picture of the new computer software piled in the boardroom under the gaze of the paper's Victorian proprietor (97).

Not all is change, of course. Some elements are constant — and one of these is the weather. Ever since the Waverley Steps have been built they have enjoyed the reputation of being the windiest spot in the whole city (8, 9) and the associated misery and drama are splendidly captured.

Fires and disasters never fail to make dramatic images — from those of the Gretna Rail disaster (45, 46) which brought so much tragedy to Leith, to the more famous blazes of recent years like the C & A fire in Princes Street (225) and the Gaumont blaze (227).

Among the most interesting pictures must be those of great buildings now torn down: the old Waverely Market (181), old Calton Gaol (190), the magnificent New Club building (215) and its cost effective but boring replacement (216), St James' Square (194) and its appallingly tasteless supplanter the St. James' Centre (196), the old Sheriff Court House building (188) — these and many more will stir memories, and, maybe, consciences.

The earlier photographs are more redolent of the techniques and composition of painting — then the more firmly established art form and some of these early images are taken from Edwardian postcards. The picture postcard was introduced in 1894 and from 1902 the Post Office permitted the use of the 'divided back' card which allowed all of the front to be used for the picture and both message and name of address to be written on the verso. Picture postcards then poured onto the market. They were far more widely used than they are today and filled many more functions than that of greetings from the seaside.

Many firms used them as advertising material and correspondence cards (VIII, IX, 27, 104) and some would seem quite inappropriate by today s standards — like the card portraying the funeral of the victims of the Gretna Rail disaster (46). But photographs were still not used in the newspapers and this was the only readily available means of obtaining a picture of a great event. Needless to say, just as in the 80s, photographs of royalty, royal visits and royal weddings were enormously popular. Some cards were used quite simply for sending straightforward messages and news — and considerably more reliably than today. All mail was, almost without exception, delivered within 24 hours and within the same area often on the same day! Further comment would be superflous.

Then there were comic cards like the one in this introduction cynically commenting on the propensity for rain in Edinburgh, and ones depicting houses (5) and castles. As the postcard craze caught on people began to collect the cards in series and it became a popular hobby as manufacturers dreamt up new series and subjects. By the end of the First World War the postcard boom was over (some of the best had been printed in Germany in fact), social conditions had changed, the postage rate had doubled and the golden age of the postcard was over. We shall, however, be forever grateful for the legacy of printed images it left.

The postcard is most often connected with leisure activity — like the view of the pier at Portobello (131) or hotels (100, 101). How people spend their

6.　Morningside Road in the snow, January 1978.

7.　Edinburgh battles with the snow: an annual event.
　　North Bridge, January 1984.

8.   Waverley Steps, January 1987.

9.   At the top of Waverley Steps, November 1981: renowned as the windiest spot in the city.

10.   A typical July day, 1985, in Princes Street Gardens!

spare time — in an age when they have far more of it than in the past — has changed out of all recognition. But a mere handful of Edinburgh's cinemas now remain of the dozens of picture palaces which attracted great crowds in the days before television and VCRs (113—125). Popular culture brought new values and activities in the 60s (126, 127) and the Forth harboured a pirate radio ship (133) in the days when, almost incredibly to young people now, there were only three or four hours of pop music on the radio in any one week!

During this century Edinburgh has changed from a city with a great industrial base of printing, papermaking, shipbuilding, engineering and craft industries to a service economy with great shops, busy offices serving not only this country but the financial centres of the world, and a bustling tourist industry with a great annual Festival at its heart. These are changes readily apparent from the most cursory look at these pages. But the photographs here do not tell the full story for there is the same old story of the confines of the covers and whole areas of activity have not been surveyed. I suppose there is little here to suggest industrial decline or conflict, little of changes in education, in health, little of the great scandals which have bubbled beneath the surface of Edinburgh life, and so on. The problem is that such things rarely make great pictures and this is a *pictorial* history of the city this century. There are, though, clearly major gaps and some of them can be plugged in Volume II.

Conversely to what I have said above, perhaps these pictures should make us grateful for what has survived in the City of Edinburgh: not just sad at what has gone. As long ago as 1911, James Bone recorded in *Edinburgh Revisited* that there was "talk of destroying Charlotte Square" while, more recently, in the 60s it was suggested that Princes Street Gardens and Queen Street Gardens be given the tarmacadam treatment and made into suitable but inelegant car parking. Indeed, one of these options was actually traded for St. James' Square thus giving birth to what one writer has so graphically described as "a hideous toad thrusting its bulk upon the cityscape".

Thankfully, there is still much of which to be proud and this modest volume will have

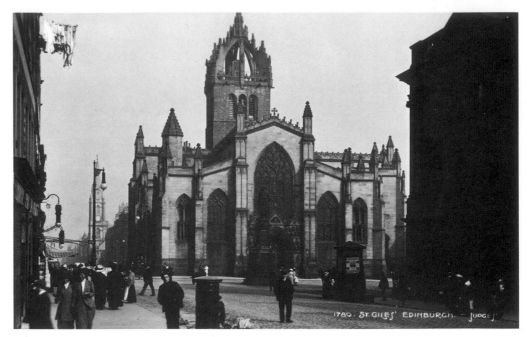

11. An Edwardian picture postcard view of St. Giles' Cathedral.

accomplished something if it makes the citizen of Edinburgh look just a little harder at what is happening all around today. It may even be worthwhile taking a few photographs and locking them away somewhere for the benefit of some 21st century observer . . .

12. Stockbridge, 1904.

DAWN
OF A NEW CENTURY

III *Rain on Princes Street*, 1913 by Stanley Cursiter
(1887 — 1976)

IV *Edinburgh from Calton Hill* by James Paterson
(1854—1932)

13.   Princes Street at Waverley Station in the 1890s. The buildings in the picture were demolished to make way for the North British Hotel.

14.   George Street, 1901.

George Street, Edinburgh.

RELIABLE SERIES.

15.   The east end of Princes Street, 1898.

16.   North Bridge — minus the North British Hotel — in the 1890s.

17.	South Bridge in the 1890s.

18.	Top of the Mound in 1901 with cable tram and elegantly dressed Edwardian ladies.

19. Maule's Corner at the west end of Princes Street at the turn of the century.

20. Corner of Leven Street and Tarvit Street — now the site of the King's Theatre — in 1900. Wilson's are offering oranges at 40 for a shilling!

21. Davidson's Mains, c. 1910. An open SMT charabanc crosses the Quality Street junction.

22. The foot of Causewayside at the corner of Fountainhall Road in 1900.

23. Easter Road at the turn of the century.

24. Statue to Queen Victoria in Leith unveiled in 1907.

VICTORIA STATUE, LEITH.
UNVEILED 12th OCT. 1907.

25. Palmerton Place.

Palmerston Place, Edinburgh

26. Decorations for the Royal visit of King Edward VII and Queen Alexandra at Waterloo Place, 1903.

27. An advertising card for John Henry ("plate, china & jewellery"), Moubray House. "Patronised by H. M. The Queen and H. R. H. The Prince of Wales".

28. Decorations in Princes Street for the Royal visit of 1911 by King George V and Queen Mary.

29. Hanover Street decorated for the Royal visit.

30. Spectacular illuminations marked the 1911 Royal visit. Maule's department store in Princes Street (later Binns).

31.   Children play pitch and toss in a Leith Street, 1909.

32.   Thirlestane Road, 1910. No pitch and toss
       in the street here!

33. Booked for stealing turnips! (circa 1911)

34. Children lined up for the photographer at the foot of the Royal Mile, 1903.

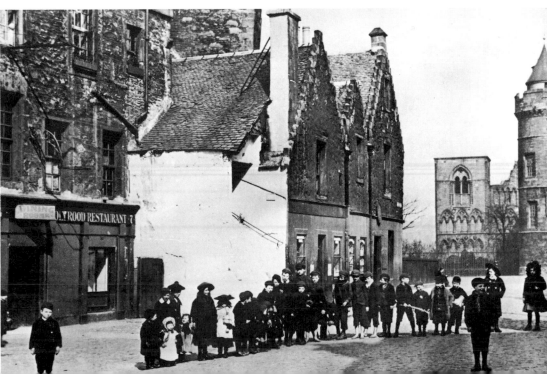

35.   The predecessor of the horse tram — the horse bus — in Trinity.

36.   The Edinburgh Northern Tramway Company's first cable car, which came into operation in 1896.

37. A horse tram at the terminus in Colinton Road. The trams could not be turned and so the horses were switched.
     This was the last horse tram route in Edinburgh and ceased in 1907.

38. Football 'specials' loading for Tynecastle at the top of Waverley Steps. Behind is the old Palace Cinema,
     demolished to make way for Woolworths (also now gone).

39.   The St. Cuthbert's delivery van, 1910.

40.   This motor van is clearly the pride and joy of its owners.

41. An Edinburgh family photographed in 1900. The glass plate was recovered from the old Patrick Thomson's photographic studio when the building on Nord Bridge was converted into the present Carlton Highland Hotel. In the first edition of this book the family was unidentyfied but is now known that the picture portays the Warwick family. Most of the male members of the family were printers in business at the time on the corner of Morrison Street and Semple Street.

42. North West Circus Place, about 1910.

North West Circus Place, Edinburgh.

43. Dean Street and Raeburn Place, 1906.

44. Free Library and Fire Station, Stockbridge, 1906.

EDINBURGH AT WAR

V *North Bridge and Salisbury Crags, Edinburgh, from the north west* by Adam Bruce Thomson (1885—1976)

VI *Dean Village* by William Wilson (1905—1972)

45.   The scene of the Gretna Rail Disaster, May 22, 1915.

46.   Funeral, with military honours, of 100 victims of the Gretna disaster at Leith.

47. An Edinburgh "Victory Tram", 1918. It sports the flag of our First war allies — Japan.

48. Graf Zeppelin over Edinburgh, August 1929.

49.   A gas bag bus on Waverley Bridge during World War 1. The bus was powered by coal gas.

50. Luftwaffe photograph of the Firth of Forth, October 2, 1939.

53. Aftermath of the German raid on the Forth Bridge, October 16, 1939. The cofffins of the dead airmen are St. Philip's Church, Abercorn Terrace, Portobello.

52. Crashed in the Lammermuir Hills, the German bomber brought down after the October 16 raid on Edinburgh and the Forth Bridge.

51. Luftwaffe photograph of north west Edinburgh, October 2, 1939.

56.   Evacuation scene at Craigentinny School, September 1,
       1939. The children, identified by luggage labels, clasp
       gas masks in brown paper parcels and boxes.

58.   Bomb damage at David Kilpatrick School, Leith, 1941.

59. An air raid shelter in Princes Street Gardens.

61. The Scottish Rest House for Servicemen, Waterloo Place, Edinburgh. In the canteen.

What do I do...
to improve my blackout?

I inspect it at night from outside my house at least once a week. I make sure that the curtains cannot flap, and that any roof lights are perfectly screened. I see that the blackout is in place before turning on the light.

I remember that the blackout is just as important in the morning, and I therefore find out the blackout times each day.

If I have been burning refuse in the garden I see that the fire is properly extinguished before dark.

Doing these things helps to ensure the safety of my district as well as my own home.

Cut this out — and keep it!

62. May 1940. Men of the Local Defence Volunteers from Greenend and district train with borrowed rifles at Hunter's Bog. The company later became G company, 3rd Battalion Home Guard Edinburgh.

63. Inside the LDV pillbox at the Dean Bridge.

64. HMS "Cossack" enters Leith with merchant seamen rescued from the German prison ship "Altmark" on February 17, 1940.

65. British prisoners liberated from the "Altmark" land at Leith.

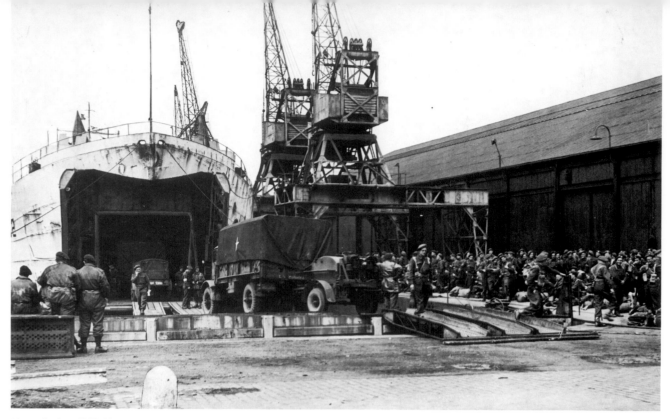

66. Spring 1945. Men and supplies embark for Norway from Leith.

67. May 1945. A German minesweeper surrenders in the Forth.

68.　Barrage balloon at the Forth Bridge.

69.   Victory celebrations, Ross Bandstand, May 1945.

70.   Winston Churchill greets the crowds in Princes Street Gardens during his visit to Edinburgh, June 1945, as part of his unsuccessful election campaign.

AT WORK

VII *Maule's Corner after Rain* by Robert Easton Stuart (1925)

VIII *Postcard of Patrick Thomson's North Bridge Store,* 1913

IX *Patrick Thomsons in the booming late 1920s*

71.   Princes Street shopfront in the 1930s.

72.   No. 8 St. Stephen Street at the turn of the century.

73. Jenners' toy department at the turn of the century.

74. The interior of Jenners in the 1950s.

75. Delivery of groceries before World War 1 at the corner of Cumberland Street and Dundonald Street.

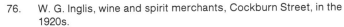

77. The cream cart outside the creamery in Morrison Street, 1925.

76. W. G. Inglis, wine and spirit merchants, Cockburn Street, in the 1920s.

78. Ramage's Dairy in the Lawnmarket. This building is now better known as Gladstone's Land.

79. Waterston's shop at 35 George Street, 1903.

80. St. Cuthbert's Dairy horse and cart at the turn of the century.

81. Ronnie O'Connor and the St. Cuthbert's Co-op horse, Ben, on one of their last rounds in Saughton Mains, January 1984.

82. The Scotmid dairy horses are retired from service, March 1985. Farrier Jim Lee and Silver are pictured with pupils from Tollcross Primary Shool.

83. Newhaven fishwives, 1903.

84. A Popular Edwardian postcard depicting Newhaven fishwives.

85. An enterprising Edwardian lemonade seller at the top of Arthur's Seat.

86.   Reporters' Room at *The Scotsman* in 1905 when the North bridge building was first occupied.

87.   Composing Room Staff outside the building, 1905.

88. A full turnout at the *Scotsman* editorial dinner, 1938.

91. Newspapers hot off the press at Waver

89. Dinner for staff who returned from the Forces at the end of the Second World War.

90. The old *Evening News* office — where the Edinburgh Festival now has its headquarters.

92. *Scotsman* van at Hampden, November 1958.

ation, 1967.

93. Princess Alexandra presses the button for the 150th anniversary edition of *The Scotsman*, January 1967.

94. Of immediate interest to tens of thousands of Edinburgh people — the Spot the Ball department, pictured in 1965.

95. The 40,000th issue of the paper, August 1971.

96. Out with the old in 1982: the linotype setting machines are removed from the building.

97. Under the baleful gaze of a Victorian proprietor of the paper, computer supplies for the new technological *Scotsman* are stored in the boardroom, May 1987.

98. North British Rubber Company staff leave its Fountainbridge Works.

99. Hot stuff at North British Rubber Company!

100. The old Queen Hotel at the corner of Queen Street and Forres Street.

101. The Roxburghe Hotel, Charlotte Square, in the 1920s.

102. A medical ward in the Royal Infirmary.

103. Pictured in 1983, the porters at the Caledonian Hotel, with, between them, more than 200 years of service, in celebratory mood on the 80th anniversary of the hotel.

104. Staff of the Victoria Legal Assurance Company in Edinburgh, 1907.

105. Ferguson's original Edinburgh Rock factory in Leith, 1969.

106. Pictured in the 1960s, the Parkside Works of Thomas Nelson, the printers.

107. The demolition of Nelson's imposing red sandstone building to make way for the Scottish Widows building.

108. Demolished 1987, the works of Morrison & Gibb, world famous printers and bookbinders.

109.   A survivor of the decline of the Edinburgh book production industry: Hunter & Foulis Ltd., Macdonald Road bookbinders, celebrated their 130th birthday, May 14, 1987.

110.   William Christie's clay pipe factory, Leith 1908.

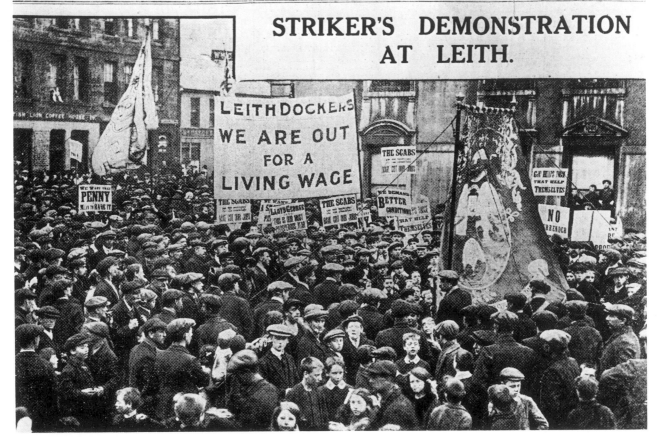

111. Demonstration by striking dockers at Leith, July 1913.

112. Edinburgh hunger marchers prepare to set out for London, December 21, 1922. Pictured at the foot of the Mound.

AT PLAY

X *Donkey Rides, Portobello Beach* by D M Sutherland
(1883 — 1973)

XI *Edinburgh Tearoom* 1913 by Stanley Cursiter (1887 — 1976)

113.　The penny matinee at The Picturedrome, Easter Road, 1923.

114.　The Alhambra Cinema, Leith Walk (demolished).

115.   The Empire Theatre, Nicholson Street, in 1925.

116.   The Ritz in Rodney Street just before its closure, September 1981.

117.   The Ritz is demolished to make way for housing, 1983.

118. Monseigneur News Cafe, Princes Street, 1963.

119. Jacey News Theatre on the same premises, 1965. A victim of the decline and ultimate extinction of the news theatre.

120. The Salon, at the top of Leith Walk, now derelict.

121. Poole's Roxy cinema.

122. The Regent, Abbeymount, closed May 1970 and now demolished.

123. The Eastway Cinema, Easter Road. Now a supermarket.

124. The foyer, Poole's Synod Hall (demolished 1966).

125. The Odeon, Clerk Street.

126. Edinburgh dance hall in the early 1950s — the era of the "Teddy Boy".

127.   Edinburgh in the 1960s: student Beatnik Ball.

128. Musselburgh Races, April 1963.

129. Shouting the odds at Musselburgh.

130. Portobello Beach at the turn of the century.

The Pier, Portobello

131. The Pier, Portobello, 1914.

132. Portobello Beach: still busy in the 1950s.

133. The pirate radio ship Radio Scotland achored in the Forth, 1966.

134. Paddle steamer "Edinburgh Castle" in the Forth.

135. Paddle steamer "Tantallon Castle" in the Forth.

136. Wallace Mercer (centre) with members of the board of Hearts, June 1982.

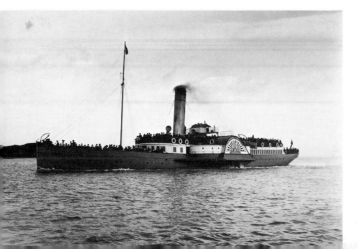

137.   Pope John Paul at the Murrayfield Stadium youth gathering, June 1982.

138. The young Queen Elizabeth and the Duke of Edinburgh in the city, June 1953.

139. The Royal Company of Archers, the Queen's bodyguard in Scotland, 1953.

140. Another wet garden party at Holyrood, July 1972.

141. The annual dinner ot the Sir Walter Scott Club, March 1966. Left to right: Alan C Frazer (secretary), Mrs. Patricia Maxwell Scott, Lady Cameron, Lord Cameron, Mrs. Frazer.

142. The Traverse Theatre's Black and White Ball at the Assembly Rooms, 1966. Left to right: Nicholas Fairbairn, Lady Primrose, Jeanette Muir and Jim Haynes, artistic director and a founder of the controversial Theatre Club.

FESTIVAL CITY

XII *Pachmann at the Usher Hall* by Stanley Cursiter
(1887—1976)

XIII *Edinburgh: North view from the Scott Monument*
(September—October 1986) by Richard Demarco

143.   Festival decorations in Princes Street, 1959.

144.   The opening of the Edinburgh Festival, 1949.

145.   The Festival Club in the Assembly Rooms, 1956.

146. Festival Edinburgh by night, 1971.

147. Councillor Macfie demands the removal of "unsightly" Festival decorations from Princes Street, 1982.

148.   "Evening News" Festival Cavalcade, 1984.

149.   Fraser's Department Store Float, 1983.

150. Participants from the Edinburgh Chinese Dance Group, 1983 Cavalcade.

151. Comedian Ronnie Corbett in a "Spot the Monkey" competitio in the Parade.

152.   Festival Fringe contingent in the 1977 Cavalcade. Andrew Cruickshank, Chairman, with administrator Alistair Moffat to his right.

153.   "The Smallest Theatre in the World", 1984 cavalcade.

154. Edward Heath conducts the European Community Youth Orchestra in rehearsal at the Usher Hall, 1980.

155. Paul Young and Rikki Fulton in the enormously successful production of "A Wee Touch of Class", Churchill Theatre, 1985.

156. Festival Fringe Sunday in the High Street, 1981.

157. The Tattoo, Castle Esplanade, 1969.

158. The set being erected in Edinburgh University's Old Quad for the acclaimed Japanese version of "Macbeth" (1986).

159. Sponsorship for the Festival from the Post Office. Jummy Logan tests the authenticity of the coins in Parliament Square.

160. Frank Delaney opens the first Edinburgh Book Festival, 1983: Chairman Lord Balfour of Burleigh to his right.

161.   The Fireworks Concert, 1985.

162.   The technical "whizzkids" behind the Glenlivet Fireworks, 1986. The concert featured 2,400 rockets and 1,000 shells — altogether 1.25 tons of fireworks.

163.   A pensive Richard Demarco, Edinburgh's art entrepreneur, photographed October 1967.
       Behind stands artist and critic Emilio Coia, outside Demarco's Melville Street Gallery.

164.   Emilio Coia makes a pavement drawing of Yehudi Menuhin, September 1971, outside
       the Scottish Television Festival Art Exhibition in Melville Street.

165.   Richard Demarco, Mary Sandeman ("Aneka") and Michael Dale judge the Fringe poster competition, 1982.

166.   The opening of *The Scotsman* Steps Art Exhibition, 1966 by actor, Laurence Harvey. Mr. and Mrs. Robin Philipson with *Scotsman* editor Alistair Dunnett at the Steps Art Exhibition, 1970.

167. Jenny Brown, assistant administrator Festival Fringe (1981), later administrator of the Book Festival inaugurated in 1983.

168. William Burdett-Coutts, founder of the successful Assembly Productions.

169. The rich diversity of the Festival — in T-shirts.

FESTIVAL PERFORMERS 1967—70

171. Patsy Fagan.

170. Mary Jane Mowat.

172. Rehearsing at the Lyceum in 1970, David Burke, Anna Calder-Marshall, John Cairney and (a young looking) John Thaw.

173. Tricia Botha.

174. Hazel McBride.

175. Paola Gassman.

176. Members of the New Philharmonic Orchestra stand in tribute to Sir John Barbirolli at the Usher Hall Festival opening concert in 1970 which Sir John was to have conducted.

177.   A general view of the opening of the 1971 Assembly.

178.   The General Assembly of the Church of Scotland 1971. Left, Lord
       Clydesmuir, the Lord High Commissioner, with Charles Fraser, the
       Purse Bearer.

THE CHANGING FACE OF EDINBURGH

XIV *The east end of Princes Street* Circa 1900 by Charles
James Lauder (d. 1920)

XV *The Enchanted Capital of Scotland* by Jessie Marion King
(1875 — 1949)

179. Pictured shortly before the turn of the century, the site of the North British Hotel and the roof of Waverley Market.

180. The new Waverley Maket, 1985.

181. The Waverley Market Dog Show, 1970.

182. Demolition of old Waverley Market, 1973.

183.	An aerial view (1970) of Portobello Power Station and Swimming Pool.

184.	Portobello Power Station comes tumbling down (July 1980).

185.   In the 1960s the open air Pool at Portobello was still a big attraction
        in the summer.

187.   The sad sight at Portobello pool in 1985.

188.   The Sheriff Court House on George IV Bridge (1931) demolished to make way for the present National Library of Scotland building.

189.   The Grassmarket pre- pedestrianisation.

190. The old Calton Gaol in Edwardian times.

191. The old Calton Gaol is demolished.

192. St. Andrew's House on the site of
Calton Gaol (1936)

193. Leith Walk (top portion demolished), St. James' Square (under demoliton) and the area now occupied by St. James' Centre, John Lewis and the Scottish Office.

194. The King James' Centre and New St. Andrew's House (1974).

195.　The view down Leith Walk in 1949 from above Register House. Most of the tenements in the picture were demolished.

196.　St. James' Square, demolished to make way for the St. James' Centre development.

197. Edinburgh Fruit Market premises, now housing the City Art Centre.

198. Bristo Street in the mid-1960s before wholesale demolition removed houses and the well known "Parker's Triangle" with its attractive mock Tudor building housing Parkers the drapers.

199. Poole's Synod Hall, Castle Terrace, latterly a cinema. Demolished 1966 for an abortive Edinburgh, Opera House development.

200. The "Wee School", Morningside, now a church.

201. Facing page, top: Elegant period houses in George Square demolished by the University to make way for modern buildings.

202. Opposite: The east end of Princes Street in 1954. Trams are already on the way out.

203. The last week of the tram. Decorated tram (No. 172) at Shrubhill.

204. The last No. 28 tram, November 1956.

205. Old horse drawn bus with the last tram at the Mound (1956).

206. The old Princes Street station at the back of the Caledonian Hotel at the turn of the century.

207. The Caledonian Hotel surrounded by scaffolding (1982) for repair and stonecleaning.

208. The Mound in the 1940s.

209. Haymarket in the 1940s.

XVI Edinburgh, 1987. *The Caledonian Hotel looking towards Edinburgh Castle*

XVII *Edinburgh Fire Brigade: Rescue work with ladders and lifesaving sling.* Reproduced from a tinted postcard (1905).

210.   Tram jam in Princes Street, 1952.

211. West end of Princes Street in the summer of 1952.

212. Tollcross, 1952.

213.   Tram line repairs, 1953.

214.   Now demolished, the elegant facade of the North British Mercantile Insurance Co.,
        64 Princes Street (1939).

215. Now demolished, the grand building of the New Club (architect, David Bryce 1834), in 1963.

216. The replacement for the old New Club building (Architect Alan Reiach, 1966).

217.   Cameron Toll, looking up Dalkeith Road, 1900.

218.   Cameron Toll Shopping Centre, 1984.

219.   The Kinetic sculpture erected at the top of Leith Walk in the early 1970s by the Corporation and the Arts Council. At the beginning of its life it changed colour with the wind direction but became subject to increasingly regular break downs and outbreaks of ridicule. Now demolished.

220.   The old Edinburgh Airport building (1969).

221.   The first flight from Turnhouse of the new BAC-111, January 1966.

DIAL 999!

222.   A manual hand-drawn pump and a modern (1974) turntable ladder at MacDonald Road.

223.   1958 Merryweather turntable ladder.

224.   A new water ladder emergency tender (1986).

225.   The big fire at C & A, Princes Street,
        November 1955.

226.   John Menzie's West Register Street fire,
        November 1968.

227. The Gaumont fire, May 1962.

228. The Edinburgh Dry Dock blaze,
Leith, 1978.

229.   Uniroyal Factory, Gilmore Park, burns, January 1962.

232.   Facing page: A seed warehouse in Leith well alight during the firemen's strike of 1978.

230.   "Green Goddess" fire engine brought out of mothballs and pressed into action by the military during the firemen's strike of 1978.

231.   Firefighting soldiers tackle a blaze at The Cauldron, West Bow, January 1978.

233.   New design of protective helmet under test (1987).

234. Seven cars, a milk float and a gritting lorry came to grief in Clermiston Road in the snow of January 1978.

235. The lounge bar Champers in Shandwick Place goes up in flames, February 1979.

236.   September 1975, and flooding brought problems for this police car in Greendykes Gardens.

237.   Willie Duff, former Hearts goalkeeper, tries to save his van, ablaze in Gray's Loan, Merchiston, June 1976.